Come Clean, Carlos

Tell the Truth

Sarah Eason

Enslow Elementary
an imprint of
Enslow Publishers, Inc.
40 Industrial Road
Box 398
Berkeley Heights, NJ 07922
USA

http://www.enslow.com

It might be useful for parents or teachers to read our "How to use this book" guide on pages 28–29 before looking at Carlos's dilemmas. The points for discussion on these pages are helpful to share with your child once you have read the book together.

Enslow Elementary, an imprint of Enslow Publishers, Inc.
Enslow Elementary is a registered trademark of Enslow Publishers, Inc.

This edition published by Enslow Publishers Inc.

Library of Congress Cataloging-in-Publication Data:
Eason, Sarah.
  Come clean, Carlos : tell the truth / Sarah Eason.
    p. cm. — (You choose)
  Includes index.
  Summary: "This title explores the story of one child who faces dilemmas about different social situations, the choices he or she makes and the consequences of those choices"—Provided by publisher.
  ISBN 978-0-7660-4306-0
  1. Choice (Psychology) in children—Juvenile literature. 2. Honesty—Juvenile literature. I. Title.
  BF723.C47E37 2014
  155.4'1383—dc23
                                        2012037704

Future editions:
Paperback ISBN: 978-1-4644-0557-0
Printed in China
122012 WKT, Shenzhen, Guangdong, China
10 9 8 7 6 5 4 3 2 1

First published in the UK in 2011 by Wayland
Copyright © Wayland 2011
Wayland
338 Euston Rd
London NW1 3BH

Produced for Wayland by Calcium
Design: Paul Myerscough
Editor for Wayland: Camilla Lloyd
Illustrations by Ailie Busby

Wayland is a division of Hachette Children's Books,
an Hachette UK company.
www.hachette.co.uk

Contents

Hello, Carlos!

Carlos is **confused**. He knows he is supposed to come clean and tell the truth, but he doesn't always understand why. Sometimes, telling fibs seems much easier, and it stops him from getting into trouble for things he has done.

Follow Carlos as he finds himself in tricky situations in which he must choose to be **honest**.

YOU
choose
too!

Fix it, Carlos

Carlos is playing soccer in the garden.

WHOOPS! His shot goes wide and smashes a flowerpot to pieces.

What should Carlos choose to do?

Should Carlos:

a tell Dad he's really sorry, and he'll be more careful next time?

b hide all the flowerpot pieces behind the garden shed?

c dig a plant up from the garden to fill the space?

Carlos, choose **a**

Of course it's bad to break things, but **accidents** happen and it's worse to lie about them. Most grown-ups get more upset about lies than accidents. It's best to be brave and come clean.

What would **YOU** choose to do?

Be kind, Carlos

Carlos's friend, James, is being really **mean** to another boy, Owen, at school.

Carlos's teacher wants to know what's going on.

What should Carlos choose to do?

Should Carlos:

a say it was some big girls who picked on Owen?

b tell the truth – James was being mean to Owen?

c pretend he doesn't know anything about it?

Carlos, choose **b**

It's really important to tell the truth if somebody is being picked on. Who wants a friend who is mean? If you tell the truth, the unkindness might stop and everyone can be friends.

What would YOU choose to do?

Don't worry, Carlos

Two of Carlos's friends are going
on a trip to a theme park.

Carlos **wishes** he was going to a theme park too.

What should Carlos choose to do?

Should Carlos:

a tell his dad that he must take him to a theme park for a **school project**?

b tell his friends he's been to a theme park and it was very boring?

C get excited about his own vacation at the seaside, doing fun things with his Dad?

Carlos, choose **C**

You don't have to do the same things as your friends to have fun. And you certainly don't need to make things up to keep them as your friends! Good friends will like you if you are honest and don't fib.

What would YOU choose to do?

Be careful, Carlos

Carlos wants to ride
his scooter around
the block on his
own, like some of
his friends do.

His dad says Carlos must wait until he is older. He is not big enough to ride on his own just yet.

What should Carlos choose to do?

c say that all his friends are allowed to go on their own, even if they are not?

Carlos, choose **a**

Don't make things up to get your own way! And don't go against someone's wishes, either. Grown-ups just want to keep you safe. Show that you can be trusted and you will be allowed to do more.

What would **YOU** choose to do?

Be true, Carlos

Carlos is really **bored**.

He starts to **doodle** on the
walls of his bedroom and makes
a mark. Yikes – what a mess!

What should Carlos choose to do?

Should Carlos:

 **a** move a poster
to cover up
his wall art?

b tell his dad
that the tooth
fairy drew
on the wall?

C say sorry and help to clean off the mark?

Carlos, choose **C**

Saying sorry is always better than telling a fib. Grown-ups want to know that they can trust you. Try to think of good ways to make up for your **mistakes**, instead of **lying** about them.

What would **YOU** **choose** to do?

Well done, Carlos!

Hey, look at Carlos! Now he knows how to make truthful choices, he's feeling much **happier**.

Did you choose the right thing to do each time? If you did, good for you!

If you chose some of the other answers, try to think about Carlos's choices to help you make truthful choices next time. Then it will be big smiles all-round!

It's always good to come clean!

How to use this book

This book can be used by a grown-up and a child together. It is based on common situations that might tempt any child to tell a lie. Invite your child to talk about each of the choices. Ask questions such as "Why do you think Carlos should tell his dad that he's drawn on his wall?"

Discuss the wrong choices, as well as the right ones, with your child. Describe what is happening in the following pictures and talk about what the wrong and right choices might be.

- Listen to grown-ups – they have reasons for saying "No," even if they don't always explain them.

- Covering up for mean people makes things worse. They can then continue being mean to even more people.

- Don't make up stories to avoid telling the truth – you just make an even bigger fib!

- Don't cover up an accident. It's better to tell the truth.

Ask your child to think about why people tell fibs. Does it make things easier? Point out what happens when the truth comes out – usually, the fibber ends up in even bigger trouble! If a child constantly tells lies, people find it hard to believe him even when he is telling the truth.

Help your child to realize through explaining and role play that grown-ups need to trust him – then they are more likely to allow children to do the things they want to do. In return, try to make sure your child feels he can own up to you if he needs to!

Glossary

accidents—when something goes wrong by mistake, such as breaking a flowerpot or a window

confused—to not understand something

doodle—to draw

fibs—lies

lying—not telling the truth

mean—to be unkind

mistakes—doing something wrong or getting something wrong

prove—to show someone that something is true

school project—a special piece of work done at school or for your homework

wishes—hoping for something

Index

Titles in the series

Library Ed. ISBN 978-0-7660-4306-0

Like all children, Carlos sometimes does things that are wrong, and doesn't come clean. He has lots of choices to make – but which are the TRUTHFUL ones?

Library Ed. ISBN 978-0-7660-4305-3

Like all children, Charlie sometimes feels a little scared. He has lots of choices to make – but which are the BRAVE ones?

Library Ed. ISBN 978-0-7660-4307-7

Like all children, Gertie sometimes plays a little dirty. We put Gertie on the spot with some tricky problems and ask her to decide what is FAIR!

Library Ed. ISBN 978-0-7660-4308-4

Like all children, Harry sometimes takes things that don't belong to him. He has lots of choices to make – but which are the HONEST ones?

32

[10]